This book
belongs to

....

Gerald Legg PhD FRES FZS is Keeper of Biology at the Booth Museum of Natural History, Brighton, England, where he regularly answers children's questions on creepy critters. He has also worked and lived in Africa, studying insects of the rainforest.

ZIGZAG PUBLISHING

Published by Zigzag Publishing, a division of Quadrillion Publishing Ltd., Godalming Business Centre, Woolsack Way, Godalming, Surrey GU7 1XW, England.

Series concept: Tony Potter
Senior Editor: Nicola Wright
Design Manager: Kate Buxton
Designed by: Nicky Linzey, Anne Wright, Chris Leishman
Illustrated by: Maggie Brand/Maggie Mundy Agency, Peter Bull, Wayne Ford/Wildlife Art Agency, Jackie Harland, Bridgette James/Wildlife Art Agency, Ruth Lindsay, Michael Steward, Steven Young

Color separations: RCS Graphics Ltd, Leeds
Printed in Singapore

Distributed in the U.S. by SMITHMARK PUBLISHERS a division of U.S. Media Holdings, Inc., 16 East 32nd Street, New York, NY 10016

Copyright © 1997 Zigzag Publishing. First published 1993.

ISBN 0-7651-9257-8
8024

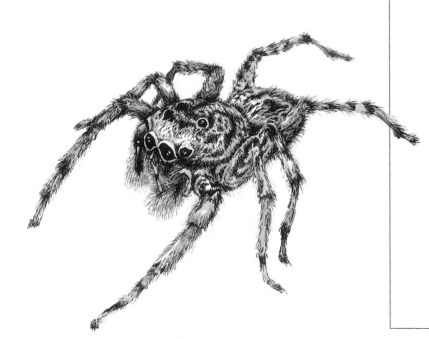

Contents

About this book

This book introduces you to the fascinating world of small creatures. These include insects, leeches, centipedes, scorpions, spiders, and snails.

Growing up

Most small animals have short lives. They may live only for one day, or for a few weeks. Many young creatures look like miniature versions of their parents. Others look very different, and go through various stages to develop into adults.

Finding food

They find food in different ways. Some hunt other creatures, while others eat plants or suck plant juices. Some find food while tunnelling through the soil.

Getting about

Creatures have different ways of getting about. Some of them fly, while others run, or wriggle through the soil. Some can even skate across the surface of water.

Hiding and showing off

Some creatures hide, while others attract attention. Some hide by blending into their background. Others attract attention by using bright colors, sounds or light.

Building homes

Most young creatures are left to look after themselves. However, some parents do care for their young. They build homes to protect the eggs and young.

Many young animals look like small versions of their parents. They simply grow into adults. Others look completely different. They develop into adults through stages.

Some young creatures that look like small adults, such as snails, grow very gradually. Others, such as insects, have a hard outer skeleton. They have to molt in order to grow.

They molt by making a new, soft skeleton beneath the hard one. The new skeleton is pumped up with air, and this splits the old skeleton. The young creature grows inside the new, hard skeleton.

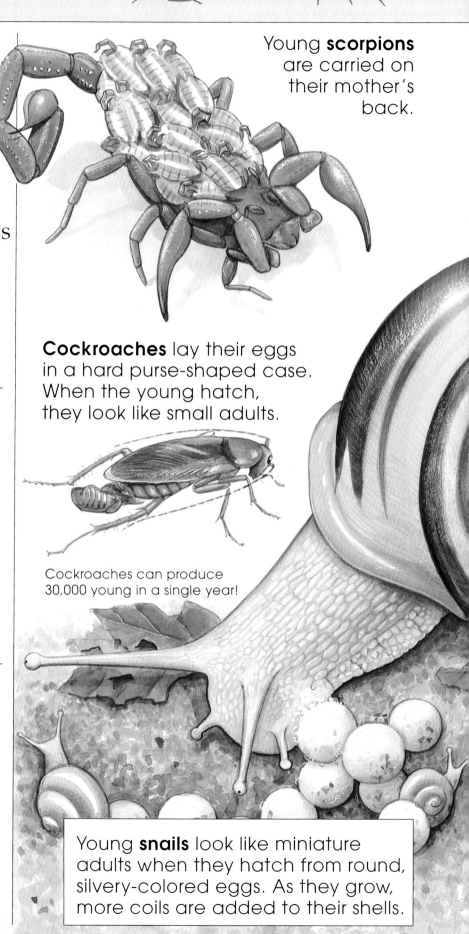

Young **scorpions** are carried on their mother's back.

Cockroaches lay their eggs in a hard purse-shaped case. When the young hatch, they look like small adults.

Cockroaches can produce 30,000 young in a single year!

Young **snails** look like miniature adults when they hatch from round, silvery-colored eggs. As they grow, more coils are added to their shells.

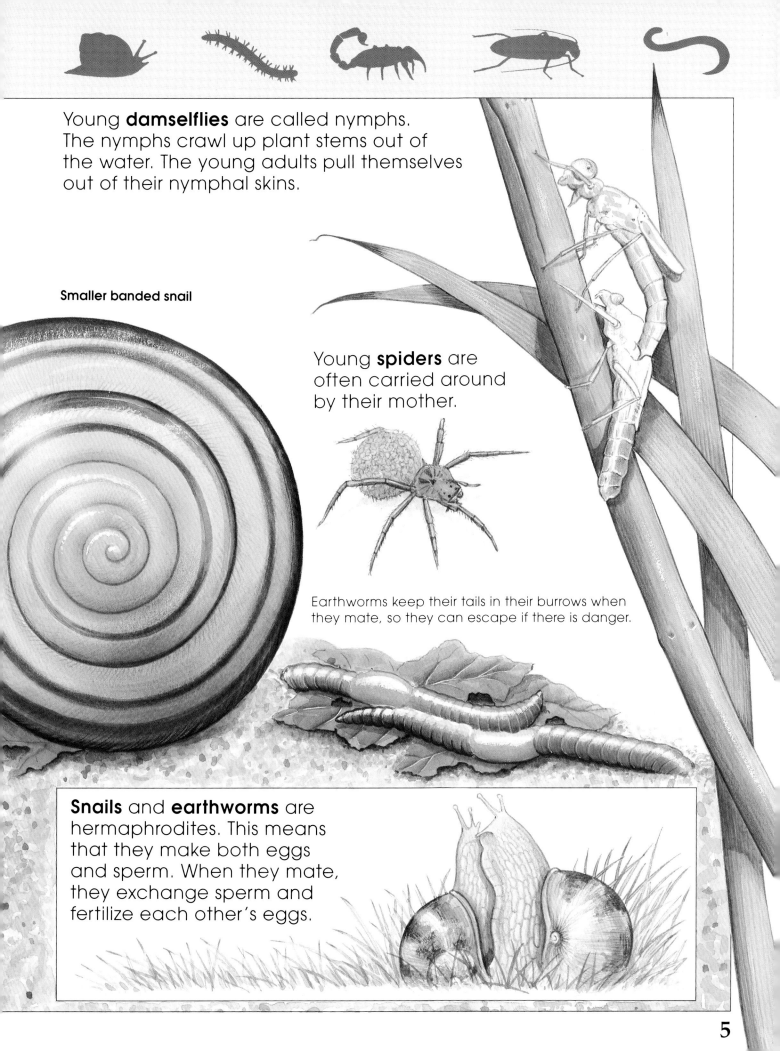

Young **damselflies** are called nymphs.
The nymphs crawl up plant stems out of
the water. The young adults pull themselves
out of their nymphal skins.

Smaller banded snail

Young **spiders** are
often carried around
by their mother.

Earthworms keep their tails in their burrows when
they mate, so they can escape if there is danger.

Snails and **earthworms** are
hermaphrodites. This means
that they make both eggs
and sperm. When they mate,
they exchange sperm and
fertilize each other's eggs.

When they are born, many young creatures look completely different from their parents. They go through several stages to develop into adults.

The young that hatch from the eggs are called larvae. A larva feeds and grows. It eventually develops into a chrysalis, which is also called a pupa. Inside the chrysalis, the larva changes into an adult. After a time, the adult emerges from the chrysalis.

The development of a larva into an adult through these stages is called metamorphosis.

Lady bug beetles and their larvae feed on aphids.

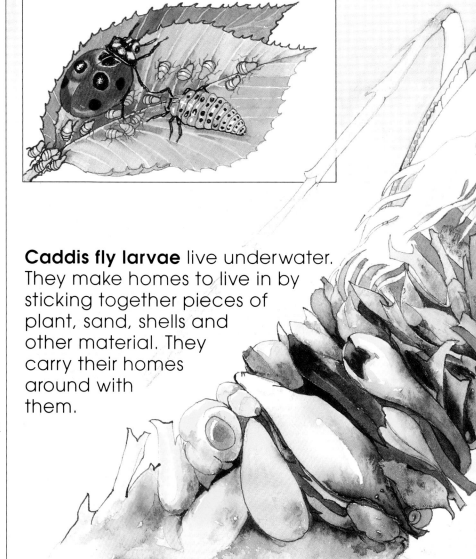

Caddis fly larvae live underwater. They make homes to live in by sticking together pieces of plant, sand, shells and other material. They carry their homes around with them.

The larvae of **butterflies** and **moths** develop into adults through metamorphosis.

This egg has been laid by a **pasha** butterfly.

This **pasha** caterpillar will turn into a chrysalis.

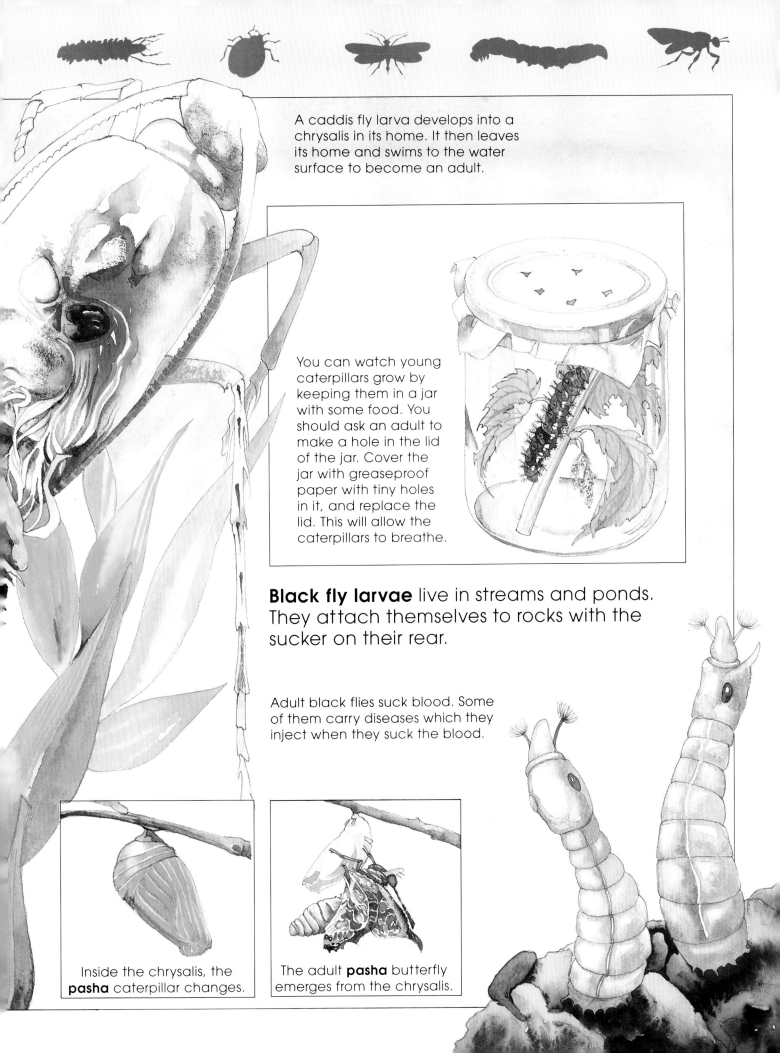

A caddis fly larva develops into a chrysalis in its home. It then leaves its home and swims to the water surface to become an adult.

You can watch young caterpillars grow by keeping them in a jar with some food. You should ask an adult to make a hole in the lid of the jar. Cover the jar with greaseproof paper with tiny holes in it, and replace the lid. This will allow the caterpillars to breathe.

Black fly larvae live in streams and ponds. They attach themselves to rocks with the sucker on their rear.

Adult black flies suck blood. Some of them carry diseases which they inject when they suck the blood.

Inside the chrysalis, the **pasha** caterpillar changes.

The adult **pasha** butterfly emerges from the chrysalis.

Hunters and trappers

Small creatures have to find food to eat in order to grow. Some of them eat the leaves, shoots, flowers, fruits and roots of plants. Many creatures even eat other creatures!

Little creatures find their food in different ways. Some of them eat rotten plants or animals, while others suck juices from plants, or even blood from animals!

Some small creatures tunnel and burrow through the soil, while others hunt for a meal on the surface of the ground. Some minibeasts even make traps in which they catch their prey.

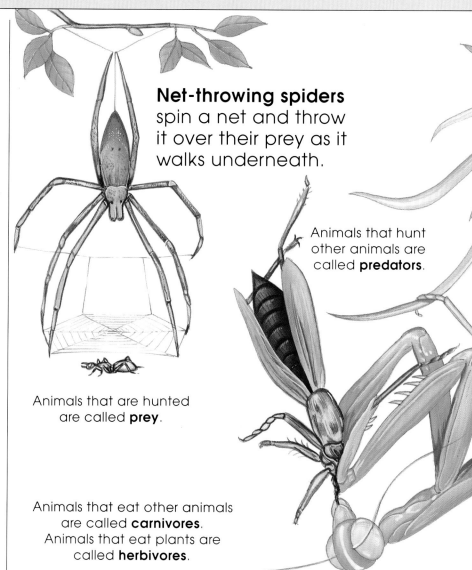

Net-throwing spiders spin a net and throw it over their prey as it walks underneath.

Animals that hunt other animals are called **predators**.

Animals that are hunted are called **prey**.

Animals that eat other animals are called **carnivores**. Animals that eat plants are called **herbivores**.

Long-jawed spiders are well camouflaged on grass as they wait for their prey to walk past.

Trap-door spiders hide in a silk-lined burrow with a trap door at the entrance. They throw open the trap door to grasp their prey.

Praying mantids are very well camouflaged. They seize their prey with their spiney forelegs and feed on it upside-down.

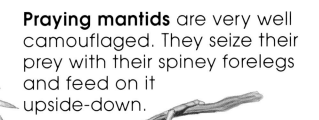

Antlion larvae lie half-hidden at the bottom of a funnel-shaped pit. They flick sand at creatures that slip over the edge of the pit, so that the tiny creatures fall down to the bottom.

Blue-black spider wasps have a loud buzz which terrifies their prey.

Euglandina rosea attacking a *papustyla* snail.

Tiger beetles are fierce hunters. They use their strong jaws to kill and cut up their prey, which includes young lizards.

Snails sometimes attack and eat other snails. If the snail has withdrawn inside its shell, the attacker will drill a hole through the shell to eat the snail.

9

Rotters, tunnellers and burrowers

Nothing lives for ever. Plants and animals die and rot away. Many feed on rotting material, helping to break it down into smaller particles.

Some of these pass into the soil, and are eaten by burrowing creatures. The particles contain nutrients which help them to grow.

Mole crickets dig burrows with their large spade-like feet. They eat the roots of plants and other insects.

Scarab beetles make balls of dung, and bury them in a tunnel where they lay their eggs. The larvae discover a pantry full of lovely food.

Mites help to break down the remains of dead plants in the soil. Some of them feed on fungi, while others hunt other mites.

Dermistid beetles help to tidy up the remains of dead animals.

Many different kinds of small creatures can be found in compost heaps. To find them, place a handful of compost in a sieve and warm it gently with a lamp for two to three days. Remember to keep the tissue paper damp.

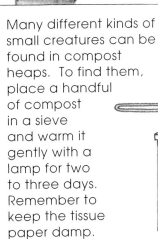

Stag beetle larvae live inside logs. They tunnel through the decaying wood for several years before they emerge as adult stag beetles.

Termites tunnel into wood or soil and build nests. These hang from trees, or are huge mounds rising from the ground.

Microscopic animals live inside termites. They break down the plant food that termites eat.

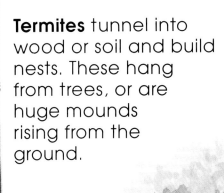

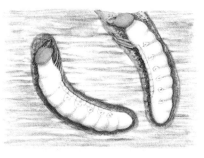

Millipedes tunnel through the soil. They eat particles of rotten material which are rich in nutrients. They also eat fallen leaves, breaking them down into smaller pieces.

Suckers

Some insects live on liquid food. They have extremely sharp mouthparts which they use to pierce the skin of an animal or the tissue of a plant.

They usually suck blood or plant juices through a sucking tube.

Fleas use the hooks and spines on their bodies to hold tightly on to the fur or skin of their hosts. Fleas can carry diseases which they inject into their hosts when they bite.

In the Middle Ages, the disease called the Black Death was spread by the rat flea. This disease killed millions of people.

Oleander Hawkmoths hover in the air like hummingbirds. Their tongues are 4.8 in. long. They use them to suck nectar from deep within a flower.

Ticks are parasites. They sink their hooked mouthparts into the flesh of their host. As they suck the blood, their round, elastic bodies swell greatly.

Aphids feed on plant juices. Their delicate mouthparts pierce the sap vessels inside a plant, and the pressure forces sweet-tasting sap into the aphid's body.

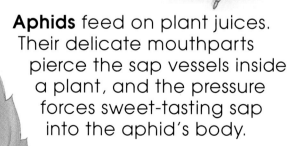

Some of the sap is passed out of the aphid as a drop of sweet fluid. This is sometimes eaten by ants.

Mosquitoes feed on blood and plant juices. Female mosquitoes have a meal of blood before they lay their eggs. Male mosquitoes suck plant juices instead of blood.

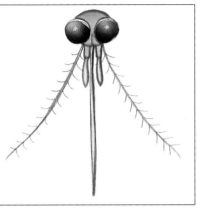

The long, needle-sharp mouthparts of a mosquito contain a sucking tube.

Female mosquitoes bite humans. A person can lose over a pint of blood in an hour.

Jungle leeches suck blood. When they have had a blood meal, their body swells.

Animals that live and feed on other animals are called **parasites**. The animals that provide a home and food are called **hosts**.

Thrips are tiny "thunder-bugs." They have mouthpieces on one side of their mouth only, which they use to suck plant juices.

Thrips are pests, feeding on corn and other crops.

Robber flies catch and stab their prey with their sharp mouthpieces. Their victim is then sucked dry.

Cochineal bugs suck plant juices. They are used to make food coloring as they are dark red.

13

Flyers

Small creatures have to get around in order to find food, a mate, and a new place to live. They also need to be able to escape from predators.

Insects use many ways of getting around. Some of them crawl and others run. Some of them jump and others wriggle. Some of them can even fly.

Most insects that fly have two pairs of wings which beat together.

Spiders are creatures that can fly but do not have wings!

A young **wolf spider** has released a long, silken thread. The wind will pluck the thread into the air, whisking the young spider away with it.

Beetles have two pairs of wings. The first pair is very tough and protects the delicate flying wings which are folded underneath when not in use.

Dragonflies chase other flying insects by rapidly beating their outstretched wings.

Emperor dragonfly

Damselflies fly by fluttering their wings. They catch other flying insects by grasping them with their legs.

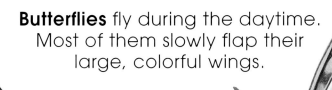

Butterflies fly during the daytime. Most of them slowly flap their large, colorful wings.

Flies are the best acrobats of the insect world. They can even land upside-down on a ceiling.

The wings of the **Painted lady** warn other insects to keep away.

Flies have only one pair of real wings. The rear wings are tiny bat-shaped objects which beat very fast.

The wings of the **swallowtail** make a noise as they clap together.

Hover flies can hover, dart backward and forward, and even fly straight upward.

Midges have one of the fastest wing beats. Some beat their wings over 1,000 times a second.

Fairy flies have delicate, feathery wings. They are one of the smallest flying insects.

Cockchafers fly at dusk. They can fly over 3 miles in search of a mate.

Crawlers and runners

Many small creatures get around by crawling or running. Some of them have lots of short legs which they use to crawl about.

Other creatures have fewer legs, but they are usually quite long. Long legs allow the creature to run about quickly.

Pseudoscorpions can run backward as well as forward! They are active hunters that crawl among decaying leaves in search of a meal.

Pseudoscorpions have long sensitive hairs on their rear to help them feel where they are going.

Caterpillars usually have plenty of food around them. As they do not need to move far to find a meal, they have short legs.

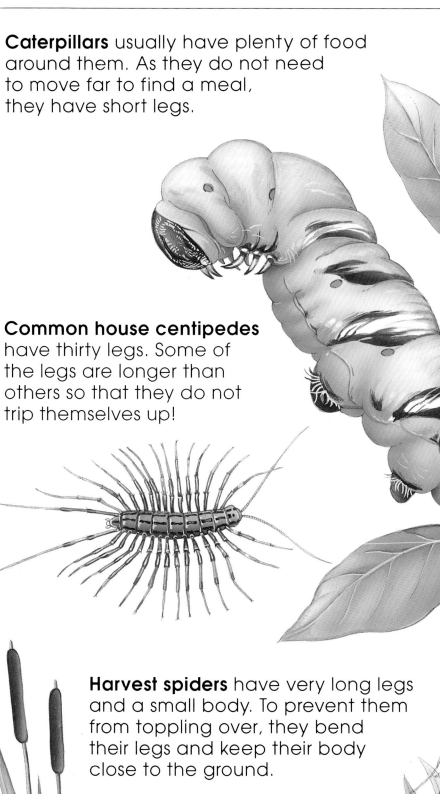

Common house centipedes have thirty legs. Some of the legs are longer than others so that they do not trip themselves up!

Harvest spiders have very long legs and a small body. To prevent them from toppling over, they bend their legs and keep their body close to the ground.

The legs of harvest spiders are not used for speed. The spiders crawl through the vegetation where they live.

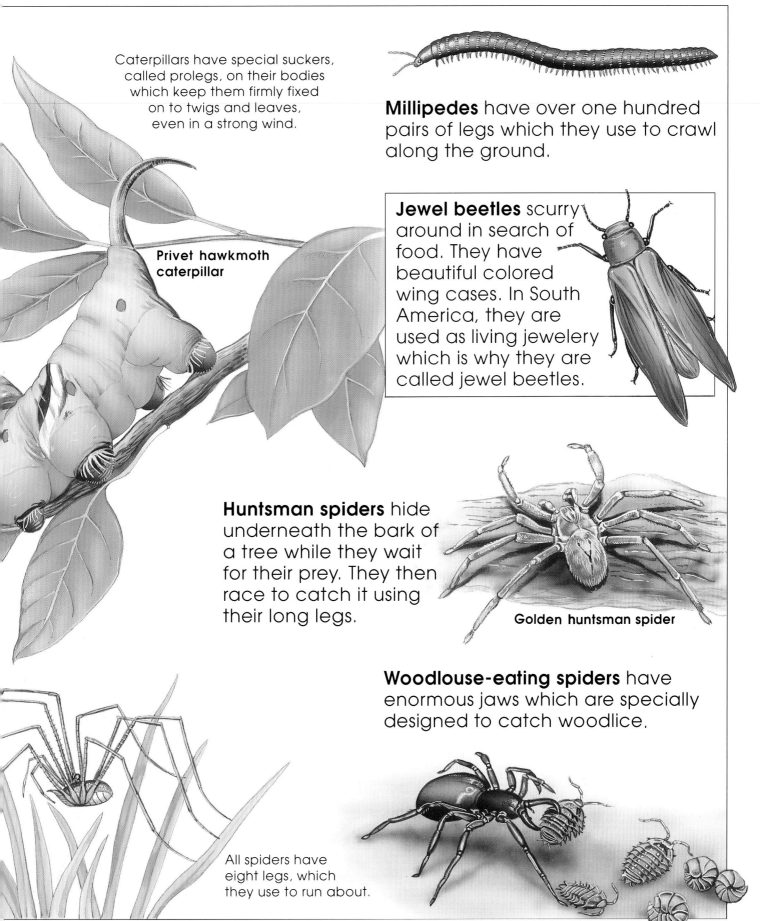

Caterpillars have special suckers, called prolegs, on their bodies which keep them firmly fixed on to twigs and leaves, even in a strong wind.

Privet hawkmoth caterpillar

Millipedes have over one hundred pairs of legs which they use to crawl along the ground.

Jewel beetles scurry around in search of food. They have beautiful colored wing cases. In South America, they are used as living jewelery which is why they are called jewel beetles.

Huntsman spiders hide underneath the bark of a tree while they wait for their prey. They then race to catch it using their long legs.

Golden huntsman spider

Woodlouse-eating spiders have enormous jaws which are specially designed to catch woodlice.

All spiders have eight legs, which they use to run about.

17

Hoppers, jumpers and skaters

Some small creatures move around by hopping and jumping. Being able to jump suddenly is a good way to catch a meal, or to escape from a predator.

Some insects skate across the surface of water in search of food or a mate.

Raft spiders stand half on the water and half on a water plant. They race across the water surface to catch their prey, which includes small fish.

Grasshoppers and **crickets** have huge back legs. They use the strong muscles in these legs to catapult themselves high into the air.

Fleas have large back legs which allow them to jump very high - well over half a yard.

Fleas jump onto animals, such as cats, where they make their home.

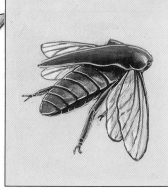

Treehoppers hop from tree to tree in search of food.

Pond skaters have waterproof hairs on their feet which help them to float on the water surface.

Springtails can spring suddenly into the air using their special "tail."

Grasshoppers attract a mate by rubbing their back legs against their front wings to make a singing sound.

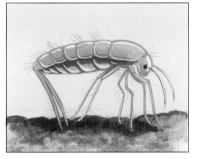 

The "tail" is tucked under the springtail's body.

The "tail" straightens suddenly, making the springtail spring into the air.

Jumping plant lice have very strong back legs which means they can jump from plant to plant.

Click beetles have a peg on their bodies. When they lie on their backs and bend, the peg pops free with a loud click, and they jump into the air.

Apple suckers are jumping plant lice which live on apple trees.

Jumping spiders have excellent sight. When they see a fly, they will leap into the air to catch it.

Whirligig beetles skate quickly across the surface of a pond in a zigzag pattern.

Slitherers and wrigglers

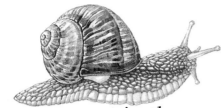

Legs can get in the way, so some creatures do not have any legs at all. They have soft bodies, and they move around by slithering along the ground or wriggling through the soil.

Earthworms make burrows which let air into the soil. They drag leaves into the burrows for food.

Leeches move along by using their suckers. They have two suckers on their bodies, one at the front and one at the rear. The one at the front has teeth as it is also their mouth.

The rear sucker sticks to the ground and the body stretches forward.

The front sucker sticks to the ground and the body is pulled forward.

African giant snail

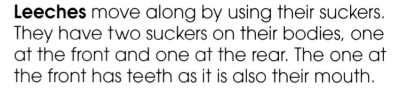

You can make a wormery by putting some earthworms and compost into a plastic bucket with small holes in the bottom. As the earthworms eat the compost, you will need to add some more to the bucket.

Earthworms burrow through the soil by eating it. They grip the soil with very small bristles along their bodies.

Slugs and snails are special creatures that slither along on a trail of slime using one foot. If you place a slug or snail on a piece of clear plastic and look at it from underneath, you will see ripples moving along the foot as the slug moves forward.

Hover fly larvae look like little leeches. They wriggle along in search of aphids which they eat.

Fly larvae hatch from eggs laid on dung. They have small legs, or no legs at all. To move about, they wriggle through their squidgy food.

Soil centipedes have up to 100 pairs of tiny legs which help them to grip the soil.

Nematodes are minute roundworms which live inside many animals and plants, and in soil. They move around by wriggling their tiny bodies.

Camouflagers

Some small creatures hide from predators or prey, while others display bright colours, make noises, or glow at night to attract attention.

Many use colors and shapes to disguise themselves. Some blend into their background, which is called camouflage. Others pretend to be fierce creatures.

Some animals use bright colors to frighten or warn their predators. Others use sound and light to "talk" to each other and attract a mate.

Assassin bug larvae look like the surrounding soil.

Peppered moths blend into the bark of the tree trunk on which they are resting.

Some peppered moths are darker. They hide on tree trunks which have been blackened by pollution.

African bush-crickets are perfectly camouflaged among the leaves.

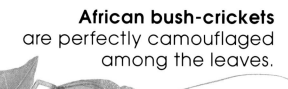

Stick insects are well hidden from predators as they look like the twigs they are sitting on.

Stick insects can be kept in a large jar as pets.

Banded snails have different shells.

The snails with pale shells live in dry, pale green grass.

The snails with dark shells live in lush green vegetation.

Flower mantids are well camouflaged as they lie in wait for their prey.

Brimstone butterflies look like the green ivy leaves that they rest on.

Crab spiders are predators that hide within flowers, waiting to pounce on visiting insects.

Tricksters

Many insects try to trick predators by using different disguises. Some of them have the same colors as creatures that are fierce or poisonous, so that predators will leave them alone.

Other insects let predators approach them, but then they give them a nasty surprise. A few even use false heads to confuse their predators!

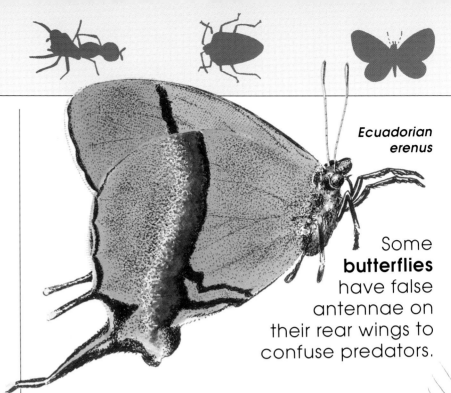

Ecuadorian erenus

Some **butterflies** have false antennae on their rear wings to confuse predators.

Tussock moth caterpillars have fine irritating hairs on their body which give predators a nasty shock!

Diadem butterflies are not poisonous but they trick their predators by flying with poisonous **African monarch** and **Citrus swallowtail butterflies**.

Citrus swallowtail

African monarch

Wasp beetles are not dangerous as they do not sting. They pretend to be wasps to trick their predators.

Copying the color of another creature is called **mimicry**. This helps to protect harmless insects from predators.

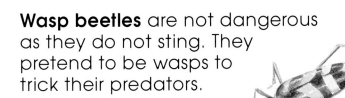

Some **jumping spiders** mimic mutillid wasps to protect themselves.

The jumping spider's rear looks like the head of a mutillid wasp.

Shieldbugs ooze a stinking liquid when they are in danger. This is why they are also called stinkbugs.

Golden-silk spiders have bright colors. At a distance, these break up the shape of the spider, making it difficult to see.

Diadem

Flashers and warners

Many creatures use bright colors to protect themselves. Some of them frighten their predators by suddenly flashing bright colors at them.

Some insects show their bright colors all the time. Predators learn that these are warning colors, telling them that the insect is dangerous.

There are only a few warning colors: black, white, yellow, red and brown. Creatures learn quickly that these colors warn of danger.

Peacock butterflies have large colorful eye spots on their wings.

Puss moth caterpillars shoot out long red tassles from tubes on their rear when they are frightened.

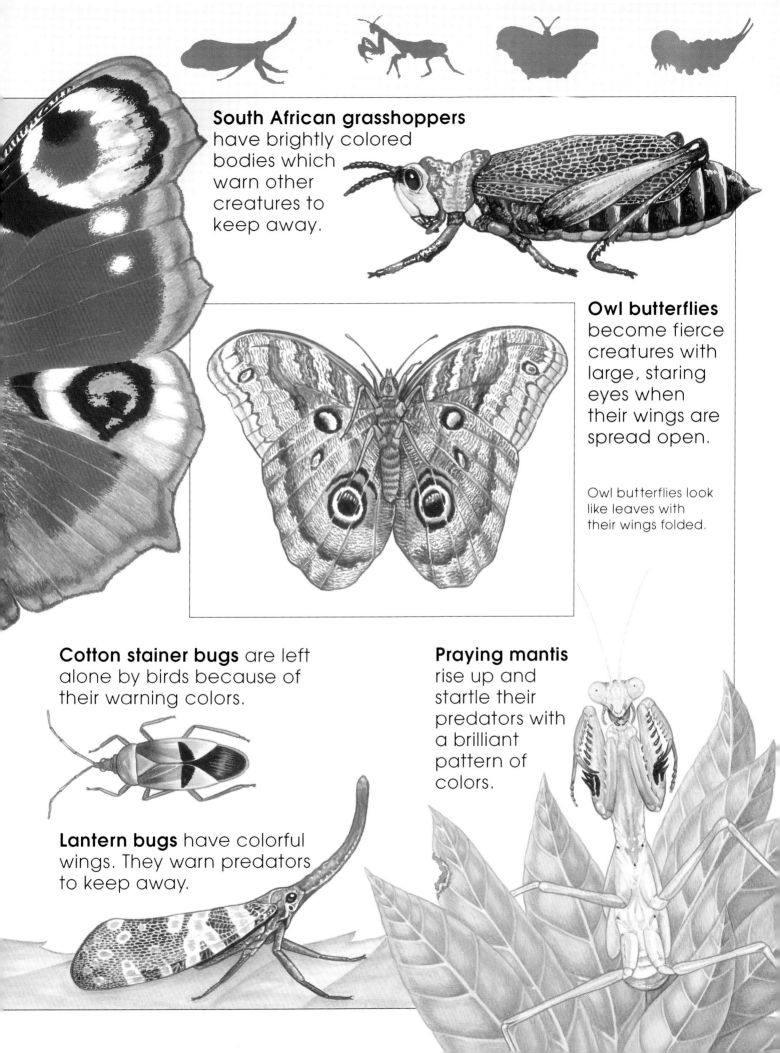

South African grasshoppers have brightly colored bodies which warn other creatures to keep away.

Owl butterflies become fierce creatures with large, staring eyes when their wings are spread open.

Owl butterflies look like leaves with their wings folded.

Cotton stainer bugs are left alone by birds because of their warning colors.

Praying mantis rise up and startle their predators with a brilliant pattern of colors.

Lantern bugs have colorful wings. They warn predators to keep away.

Singers and glowers

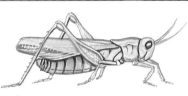

Many creatures use sound to attract a mate, or to warn off predators. Some of them make sounds during the day. If you walk through a field or a forest, you may hear all kinds of chirps and buzzes.

Many insects make sounds at night, while others use light to attract a mate. The males or females glow in the dark, and their mates are attracted to them.

Katydids sing their repetitive song "katydid, katydidn't" at night. They sing by rubbing their left front wing against a ridge on the right wing.

Katydids and other crickets have ears on their legs.

Tree crickets make thousands of piercing chirps without stopping. Some tree crickets can be heard 1 mi. away!

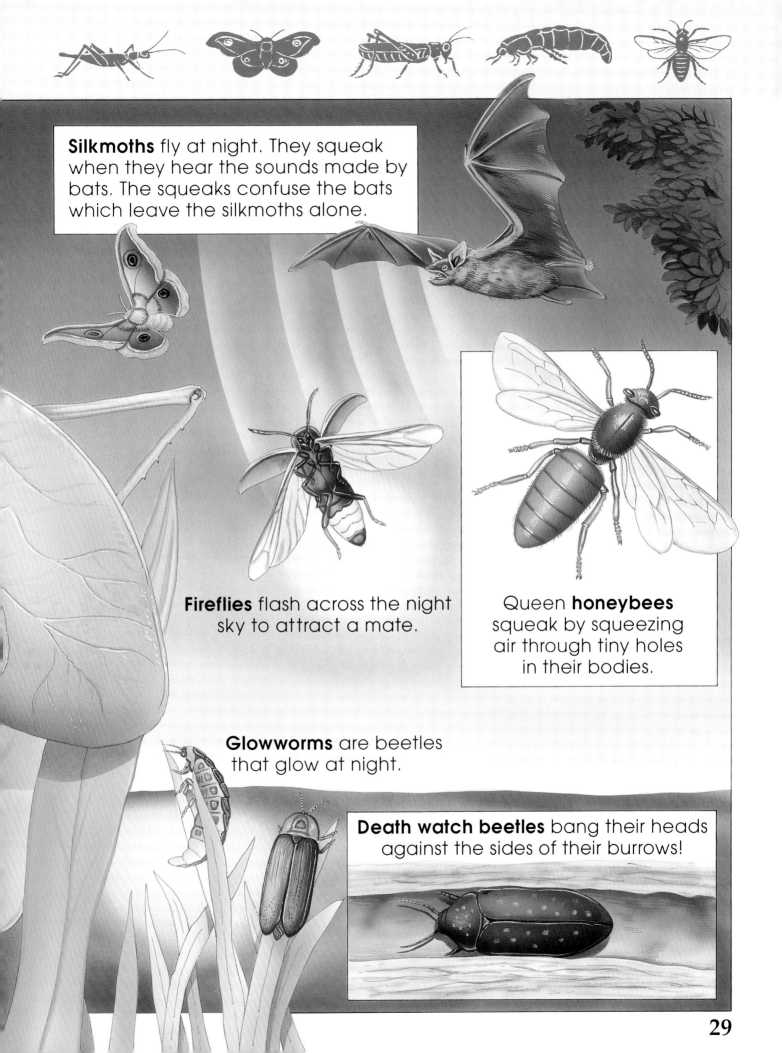

Silkmoths fly at night. They squeak when they hear the sounds made by bats. The squeaks confuse the bats which leave the silkmoths alone.

Fireflies flash across the night sky to attract a mate.

Queen **honeybees** squeak by squeezing air through tiny holes in their bodies.

Glowworms are beetles that glow at night.

Death watch beetles bang their heads against the sides of their burrows!

Carers

Most creatures leave their young to look after themselves. Many of the young starve to death, or are eaten by predators. To overcome this, many eggs are laid.

Some creatures care for their eggs and young, so fewer eggs need to be laid. Insects such as female ants or bees work together to provide shelter and food for their young, giving them a better chance of survival.

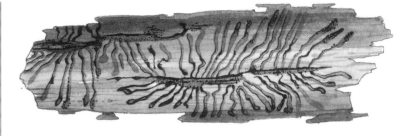

Look at the bark of fallen trees and see if you can find the tunnels of bark beetles.

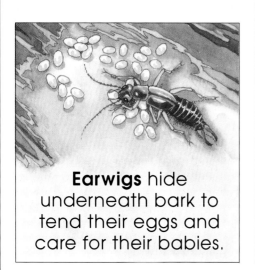

Elm bark beetles tunnel under the bark of a tree where they lay their eggs.

Termites live as a family in a huge nest. The king and queen live in the royal chamber. The queen's body swells to a huge size as she lays her eggs inside it. She can lay 30,000 eggs a day.

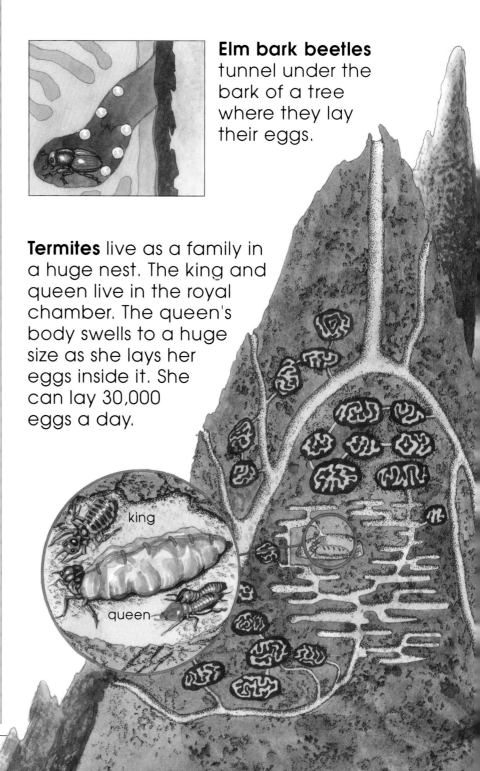

king

queen

Earwigs hide underneath bark to tend their eggs and care for their babies.

Tailor ants make nests out of leaves. The workers sew the leaves together with silk made by the saliva glands of the larvae!

Pseudoscorpions carry their eggs on their bodies and feed them "milk." They look after their eggs and young inside a tiny nest made of silk.

Queen **bumblebees** build a wax honeypot in the nest where they lay their eggs, so they have plenty of food. They care for the young on their own.

Sandwasps catch and sting a caterpillar. This sends it to sleep. They put it in a burrow in the sand, and lay an egg on it.

When the egg hatches, the larva feeds on the sleeping caterpillar.

Oak gall wasps lay their eggs on the rib of an oak leaf. The rib swells and forms a gall which is a safe home for the larvae that grow inside it.

Galls come in all shapes and sizes. The aleppo gall is used to make special permanent ink which is used by banks.

31